FLORIDA KEYS PORTS OF CALL

by
THOMAS A. HENSCHEL

A BOATING AND TRAVEL GUIDE TO
THE FLORIDA KEYS FROM
PORTS OF CALl PUBLISHING

A sportfishing boat sets out for bluewater fishing.

Sunsets are a cause for celebration in the Keys.

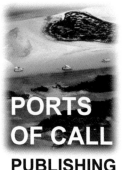

PUBLISHED BY
PORTS OF CALL, LLC

CONTACT:
info@cruisingfloridakeys.com

By THOMAS A. HENSCHEL
Publisher

AERIAL PHOTOGRAHY
Joe Melanson

DESIGN & GRAPHICS
Thomas A. Henschel

ON THE COVER
A seaplane departing Key West carries
visitors to Fort Jefferson in
the Dry Tortugas.
*Photo Seaplanes
Of Key West*

DEDICATION
To my first granddaughter Zoe, who I am looking
forward to introducing to the Florida Keys

Third Edition

The Hemingway look alike contest held in Key West. Photo Florida Keys News Bureau

The Sombrero light marks a popular location for diving and snorkeling.

CONTENTS

The "Sandbar" on a weekend at Whale Harbor Channel.

INTRODUCTION

The Florida Keys represent a truly magical destination for the vacationer, the cruising boater, scuba diver and snorkeler, sportfishing fan or the watersports enthusiast. The magic includes an endless variety of activities, shops, resorts, vacation attractions and fine restaurants. The Keys also offer the worlds' finest fishing and diving or snorkeling over coral reefs that can only be described as spectacular.

This book highlights dozens of the Keys in spectacular aerial images that depict some of the most popular and scenic vacation destinations and ports of call throughout this chain of islands. The gallery of aerial photographs found within follows the Keys from their northern reaches near Miami in Biscayne Bay to their end at the Dry Tortugas.

An angler releases a trophy bonefish.
Photo Hawk's Cay Resort

THE UPPER KEYS

Key Largo is known as the diving capital of the world and the showcase of this island lies just offshore, the John Pennekamp State Park which is the first underwater

Continued on Page 13

Offshore fishing in the Keys is considered among the finest for action and trophy fish in the world.

The old and new spans of the
Seven Mile Bridge with Pigeon
Key in between.

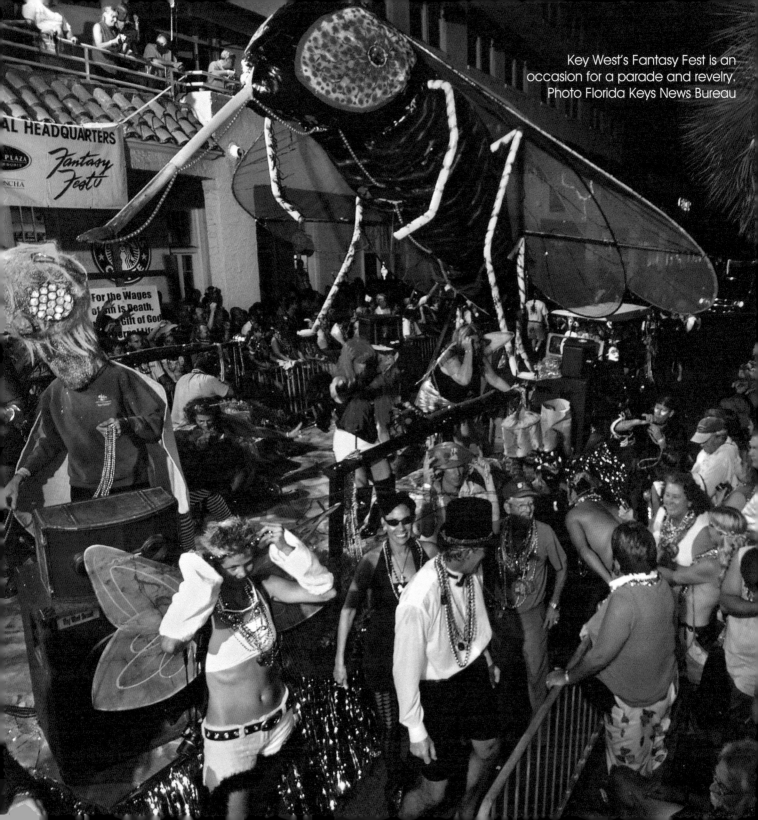

Key West's Fantasy Fest is an occasion for a parade and revelry.
Photo Florida Keys News Bureau

Continued from Page 9

preserve in the country. Here scuba divers and snorkeers have the opportunity to view more than 600 species of tropical fish and a wide variety of types of coral. At the park, which is part of the Florida Keys National Marine Sanctuary, visitors can take part in canoe and kayak trips, picnicking, camping, fishing, boating and many other activities. A state operated marina is also part of the park.

Key Largo is a sprawling region comprised of strip malls, dive centers, colorful shops and numerous marinas. In the Rock Harbor area of Key Largo you will find the original African Queen, made famous by Humphrey Bogart and Katherine Hepburn in the movie of the same name.

Farther down Key Largo is the small community of Tavernier. Reportedly, this town was named by the sailors who visited there in bygone years and found plenty of taverns where they could quench their thirst after voyages. The town

Continued on Page 18

The *Western Union* at its berth in Key West's Historic Seaport.

People are not the only ones who enjoy boat rides.

Kayaking is a popular pastime on the Keys protected waters.

The Ceaser Creek passage providing Atlantic Ocean access from Biscayne Bay in the northern Keys.

The Keys offer outstanding waters for sailing, both in the Gulf of Mexico and the Atlantic Ocean.

Kayaking over the pristine waters of the Keys.
Photo Hawk's Cay Resort

Continued from Page 13

remains interesting as many of the turn-of-the century homes have been restored.

The upper Keys with its wide spectrum of watersports, vacation rentals, resorts, activities, shopping and attractions remains one of the most popular places to vacation in Florida and the country.

MIDDLE KEYS

According to history, the early Spanish explorers that visited the coast off of Islamorada noticed a purple hue from the lavender shells of sea snails and dubbed this Islamorada, which translates into "purple isles" in Spanish. Today, Islamorada is best known as being the sportfishing capital of the world. Here there are literally hundreds of charter boats which can transport the angler to offshore waters in search of billfish (marlin and sailfish), dolphin, wahoo, kingfish and a wide variety of reef fish, or to the back country where snook, redfish, tarpon, bonefish and permit are the favorite quarry for flats fishing.

The Village of Islamorada actually takes in several communities and keys. There are numerous shops and restaurants throughout this section of the islands, as well as famous resorts that are Keys landmarks. Dining and shopping opportunities abound, and while the emphasis may be on fishing, the snorkeling and diving is also outstanding.

Indian Key and Lignumvitae Key, between Upper and Lower Matecumbe Keys, have become part of the state park system, and both feature interesting histories. South of Lower Matecumbe Key, Long Key State Park has one of the finest beaches in the Keys.

In the heart of the Florida Keys is Marathon, reportedly

Continued on Page 22

A Key West schooner
under full sail.

The lighthouse in the Dry Tortugas on Loggerhead Key.

Palm trees, the ocean and a sandy beach add up to an ideal Keys vacation.

Continued from Page 18

named for the "marathon" task undertaken by workers building Henry Flagler's Overseas Railway. Marathon is located on Key Vaca which likely received its name through the Spanish phrase Cayos de Vacas, or cow keys. This probably referred to the large numbers of manatees or sea cows that were found in the surrounding waters. Marathon is a bustling community with a wide choice of restaurants, activities, stores and shops, bars and fast food outlets.

LOWER KEYS
AND KEY WEST

The hustle and bustle of Marathon sharply contrasts with the less populous lower Keys where the atmosphere is laid back in true Conch style. Bahia Honda Key boasts one of Florida's finest state parks where there is a marina, delightful beaches and many activities for the visitor. Nearby Big Pine Key, named for its stands of pine forest, is home to the National Key Deer Refuge and the Great White Heron National Wildlife Refuge. This area is a naturalist's paradise with hiking, beachcombing, bird watching and kayaking being favorite pastimes. Fortunately, many of the outlying keys remain pristine and largely untouched.

Offshore of Ramrod and Summerland Keys is one of the Keys most popular diving and snorkeling sites, Looe Key. The coral formations found on this part of the reef are incredible and fish life abounds.

For many traveling by car, Key West represents the end of the journey. As one of the most visited destinations in the country, Key West offers something for everyone. The dining and entertainment options are staggering and are available nearly around the clock. The widest range of Key West vacation rental accommodations ranging from motels and resorts to homes and guest houses. While being a major tourist destination, this city also has its share of history and culture. There are numerous museums and a great number of galleries featuring works created by local artists. The sunset celebration at Mallory Square is a must. A visit to Key West can be as exhausting or relaxing as your taste dictates.

Beyond Key West are the Dry Tortugas and Fort Jefferson that can only be visited with your own boat, ferry service or by seaplane charter. This historic fort is a marvel in itself and the surrounding waters are perfect for diving, snorkeling and fishing.

The Florida Keys and their famed waters provide an unparalleled diversity that make them one of the world's finest vacation destinations.

PUBLISHER'S NOTE...

This new travel and boating guide joins others in the series including *The Bahamas -- Abaco Ports of Call, The East Coast of Florida Ports of Call, Southwest Florida Ports of Call* and *The Chesapeake Bay Ports of Call.* Contact *info@cruisingfloridakeys.com*

Alligator Light marks Alligator Reef offshore of the lower end of Upper Matecumbe Key. The reefs marked by lights usually represent favorite snorkeling and diving sites.

Florida Bay, the Gulf of Mexico side of the Keys, consists of winding waterways and countless small mangrove islands. The backwaters are inviting to the fishermen exploring these waters.

World championship offshore powerboat racing in Key West. Photo Florida Keys News Bureau

FISHING THE KEYS

by Harlan Franklin

I am a dyed-in-the-wool fisherman and my introduction to the Florida Keys could not have been more impressive. At first light Key West was barely in sight on the horizon after an overnight sail from Marco Island. As exciting as that sight was, another sight was just as attention grabbing. Spanish mackerel were everywhere, in all directions, as far as I could see. Thousands of them... leaping skyward, slashing through schools of silvery baitfish, turning the Gulf of Mexico's calm surface into a foamy sea of activity. It was a simple matter to toss a jig out and snare a fresh mackerel for supper.

Fishing and diving are what the Florida Keys are about. It doesn't matter where in the Keys you are, there is good fishing nearby. If you tie up at a marina, chances are you can watch snapper, jack, barracuda and no telling what else swimming around your boat... if you're on the

Continued on Page 29

Redfish, sea trout, bonefish and permit are commonly targeted species by anglers.

FLORIDA KEYS FISH SPECIES

INSHORE & THE FLATS

Bonefish
While not considered table fare, bonefish are found in schools year around on the countless miles of flats found in the Keys. Known for blistering runs once hooked, this is a popular species sought by sporting anglers using fly rods or light spinning tackle. Bonefishing entails stalking the fish and then accurately sight casting a fly or a small jig. A less sporting approach is the use of small chunks of conch, crabs or shrimp.

Barracuda & Sharks
Both barracuda and a variety of sharks can provide exciting action on the flats with light tackle. Sharks can be spotted cruising the flats in search of food and will often swallow up cut bait and even a properly presented fly. Barracuda will hit live baits, tube lures and a variety of other artificial baits. Both can provide an exciting experience on light line.

Snapper & Grouper
There are several species of each of these fish groups which are found in both inshore and offshore waters.

Continued from Page 27

hook in an anchorage, the fish may not be so visible, but they are there.

The wide variety of fish available, both the tasty types and the sporty types, is hard to imagine. Dragging a spoon or jig behind your boat is very likely to hook a mackerel or kingfish. From bridges you'll find a wide variety of fish.

Snapper, small grouper, bar jack, and mackerel all frequent the many channels with bridges providing fishing access. A selection of D.O.A. lures, small jigs, or live shrimp all work great for these fish. Those wishing to fill their coolers might want to seek out a professional guide for a trip to the reef, where the prospects of multiple fish catches are common. Chances are your catch will include a limit of prized and great tasting yellowtail snapper.

Sportfishing opportunities in the Keys are wide and varied. Bonefish, properly described as the gray ghost of the flats, can be found the length of the Keys. So can the wily permit, but these prestigious gamesters are more plentiful around the flats west of Key West. Barracuda and sharks also roam the shallow flats and both provide some interesting moments when the more sought after species become scarce. All these species will take a properly presented lure or fly. Even though a guide is not necessary, it is recommended. In selecting a guide for any purpose in the Keys, make inquiries among other anglers and ask for suggestions as to which guide to hire.

The Keys have become synonymous with tarpon. During spring and summer, fly fishermen line the edges of the flats and banks waiting for the silver king to appear. And they will appear, on both the Atlantic and Gulf and in between, all up and down the Keys.

Tarpon will first appear in large numbers early in the year,

Continued on Page 30

Yellowtail snapper.

Continued from Page 29

usually in January, in Key West's Northwest Channel. It is the opinion of many seasoned fishermen that Northwest Channel is the best place anywhere to catch a tarpon, better even than famed Boca Grande Pass upstate.

The odd thing is, the Keys are not widely thought of as a billfishing destination. They should be. Both sailfish and blue marlin are caught in surprising numbers. They can be taken on the Atlantic side anywhere along the Keys, from Key Largo to the Marquesas. The sailfish are usually found just off the reef and the marlin farther out. The waters off Key Largo have a great fall run of sailfish, as does Islamorada, Marathon and Key West.

Twenty miles off Key West, a drop off called "Wood's Wall" is becoming well known as a marlin hotspot. Both sails and marlin are caught year around, though both have their hot periods. A recently rejuvenated and exciting fishery is for broadbill swordfish. Night fishermen drifting live bait or squid in the deep water outside Wood's Wall are finding excellent numbers of swordfish. Best attempt this on nights that are calm, clear and with little moonlight.

Fish, eating fish, catching fish, or just looking at fish... it's all a big part of the Florida Keys. When you arrive in the Keys, think like a native.

Think fish.

Snapper are one of the most popular and abundant fish common to these waters. Pan-sized grey snapper, yellowtail, mangrove and the larger mutton fish are all great sport and likewise served on the table.

Grouper range from those that can fit in the pan to others which may not fit in a cooler. Adjust the size of your bait accordingly. Small jigs or chunks of cut bait work well. For grouper, try larger jigs in deeper waters with plastic tails. Trolling silver spoons or a diving plug is also effective.

MACKEREL
Spanish mackerel are easily caught trolling a small spoon or feather. They are common to the inshore waters and their larger cousins, the king mackerel will be found offshore.

OFFSHORE
MARLIN & BILLFISH
Blue and white marlin, as well as sailfish, are highly sough after bluewater species. Florida Keys blue marlin can tip the scales at hundreds of pounds. It is specialized fishing, but open to any seaworthy boat. Most used are large trolling lures or a bait, such as a rigged mackerel.

TUNA, DOLPHIN & WAHOO
These are three highly sought after species which not only provide great sport, but also excellent eating. All are most commonly caught trolling artificial baits, such as feathers, high speed trolling lures or plugs and spoons.

The manatee, or sea cow, is found in Florida waters including throughout the Keys. Fortunately, their numbers have been rebounding in recent years.
Photo Visit Florida

Snorkeling over a Keys reef.

BENEATH THE SEAS

South Florida and the Keys are home to the only living coral reef in the United States and this distinction has made this group of islands the world's most visited diving location.

Encompassing an area largely from Key Biscayne through the Dry Tortugas, this reef system is incredibly complex and equally beautiful. As such a unique and valuable natural and recreational asset, it has been designated as the country's only marine preserve, the Florida Keys National Marine Sanctuary.

Different areas of the Keys coral reef also have their own unique characteristics. Some are known for their great abundance of fish life and others for spectacular coral formations, or a wide diversity of marine life.

Wreck diving is additionally extremely popular.

Best of all the reef is accessible to both divers and snorkelers alike. For even the most advanced diver, the Keys provide challenging diving, and for the novice snorkeler, they are equally captivating.

Key Largo has named itself the dive capital of the

Continued on Page 35

There are many dive operators throughout the
Keys making daily trips to spectacular reefs.

Continued from Page 33

world and here you will find more dive shops for the area
than anywhere else. The famed John Pennekamp Coral
Reef State Park is located in Key Largo and additionally
another underwater namesake, the Statue of Christ in
the Abyss. This statue of Christ, with outstretched and
welcoming arms, may be one of the single most photo-
graphed attractions by divers. While Key Largo is a hub
of much of the diving activity it certainly is not limited
to this island. Nearly every community in your travels
through the Keys have dive shops that offer daily boating
tours, instruction and equipment rentals.

Divers and snorkelers (above) enjoying the
sights over the reef at the Sombrero Light
offshore of Marathon. The statue of
Christ is a widely visited underwater
attraction off Key Largo.

The Keys are home to the only living reef in the country and teem with fish life.

Biscayne Bay &
The Northern Keys

The Cape Florida Lighthouse
on Key Biscayne.

VIRGINIA KEY

Miami Marine Stadium was once a showpiece of Virginia Key, but Hurricane Andrew laid the facility to waste and it has unfortunately never been rebuilt. It was once the site of boat races and waterfront concerts. It is an ideal anchorage because of its shelter from all directions, however, anchoring here is reportedly strongly discouraged. Hopefully, some plans are being made for this valuable resource. Again, Virginia Key is an excellent staging stopover for cruisers heading to the Keys or to the Caribbean.

Rickenbacker Marina is owned by the city of Miami and may have slips available for overnighting. It's advisable to check availability in advance.

NAVIGATION

Virginia Key is the first island off the ICW after passing the Port of Miami and the Miami River. The marina is easily accessed from the Intracoastal just before approaching the Rickenbacker Causeway. There is a mooring field just off the entrance to the marina and only sailboats qualify to utilize these moorings. Check with the marina harbormaster on your VHF if you plan to take up a mooring.

The southern side of Virginia Key does offer prospects for anchoring, which would offer protection during northerlies, but it is open to any winds from the south.

ASHORE

The southern shores of Virginia Key are heavily used as a recreation center for all sorts of activities and this is part of the city's park system. On weekends you will find large fleets of catamaran sailors and windsurfers taking advantage of the wide open waters off the beach. This is an extremely popular spot for picnics, jogging, swimming and sunbathing. The smaller sailboats can be launched from the beach and there are paved trails along the entire beach.

The Rusty Pelican, a longtime favorite dining establishment, also has one of the most spectacular views of downtown Miami, especially after sunset. The food is outstanding and the restaurant has enjoyed years of success. Another restaurant adjacent to the marina is the Madfish House which has an adjoining Tiki bar.

Also on the grounds of the marina complex is a small bait and tackle shop, a convenience store, a boat ramp and boat rentals. Dry storage for trailerable boats occupies much of the remaining property.

VIRGINIA KEY

Rickenbacker Causeway

ICW

Madfish House

Moorings

VIRGINIA KEY

Rickenbacker Marina

Rusty Pelican Restaurant

Boat Ramp & Boat Rentals

Convenience Store

Tiki Bar

NOT TO BE USED FOR NAVIGATION
Use as a reference only. Consult recommended charts for navigation.

N

CRANDON PARK
KEY BISCAYNE

Crandon Park Marina on Key Biscayne is owned and operated by Miami-Dade County and again transient slips may be hard to come by at this port of call. Because of its popularity the majority of slips are occupied by boats on long term leases. This is a large facility and up-to-date by any standards. It is part of a huge park complex that occupies much of Key Biscayne and it encompasses beaches, miles of trails and bike paths, tennis courts and much more. All this is found in an immaculately kept tropical setting that makes for widely varied recreational opportunities.

NAVIGATION

There are three approaches to reach Crandon Park Marina depending upon the direction you are traveling. From the north, access can be made off the ICW skirting the Virgina Key beach and passing this key's southernmost tip. There are shoals here, but they are marked. It is possible to reach the marina from the ocean through Bear Cut, however, this passage is only recommended for smaller boats because of shoaling off the channel entrance and the limitations of a 16-foot vertical clearance fixed bridge. From the south and Biscayne Bay, a well-marked channel leads through Bear Cut and to the marina.

ASHORE

The marina offers both gasoline and diesel fuel and a small ship's store can provide ice, sodas, snacks, bait and tackle. There is a large parking lot and launch area for the many trailer boaters who utilize this facility. Also on the premises is a boat rental operation, a diving center and a fleet of charter boats. Sundays on the Bay Restaurant is an extremely popular restaurant located on the marina grounds.

Besides all the activities available within Crandon Park, the Miami Seaquarium is a short distance away. This attraction has provided entertainment for thousands of visitors over the many years of its existence.

A short ride away you will find the Village of Key Biscayne and here you can dine at a number of fine restaurants or enjoy the luxury of an oceanfront hotel. Grocery stores, gourmet markets and other shopping is available in this small, but elegant community.

Key Biscayne and Virgina Key represent outstanding cruising destinations, and making reservations for dockage is worth the effort.

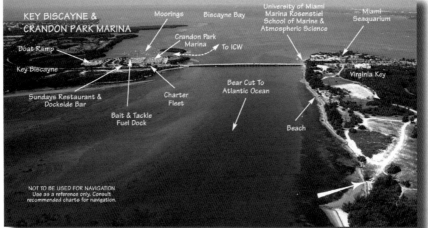

KEY BISCAYNE & CRANDON PARK MARINA

Boat Ramp
Key Biscayne
Sundays Restaurant & Dockside Bar
Bait & Tackle Fuel Dock
Moorings
Biscayne Bay
Crandon Park Marina
To ICW
Charter Fleet
Bear Cut To Atlantic Ocean
University of Miami Marina Rosenstiel School of Marine & Atmospheric Science
Miami Seaquarium
Virginia Key
Beach

NOT TO BE USED FOR NAVIGATION
Use as a reference only. Consult recommended charts for navigation.

CAPE FLORIDA

KEY BISCAYNE

The historic Cape Florida lighthouse, towering over the beaches of eastern Key Biscayne, holds the distinction of being the oldest standing structure in Miami-Dade County. The first lighthouse on the site was destroyed by Seminole Indians during the Second Seminole Indian War and the second tower which stands today was completed in 1846. The lighthouse is the signature attraction of the Bill Baggs Cape Florida State Park that is one of the most popular parks in the state. This park is also the home to an incredible beach that was once named as one of the top ten in the country. No Name Harbor within the park's grounds is widely utilized by boaters for day trips and overnighting with a modest fee for both.

the anchorage is the perfect spot for spending the night before setting out for the Keys or the Bahamas. This harbor offers a safe refuge for waiting out poor weather, and offers protection from all wind directions. Another potential anchorage is found to the north of the harbor on the western shore of Key Biscayne. It provides fair shelter and again is a good stepping off point for cruises involving Atlantic routes.

KEY BISCAYNE, CAPE FLORIDA
KEY BISCAYNE
Miami Beach
No Name Harbor
Village of Key Biscayne
Bill Baggs Cape Florida State Park
Cape Florida Channel
Cape Florida Lighthouse
CAPE FLORIDA
Shoals
NOT TO BE USED FOR NAVIGATION
Use as a reference only. Consult recommended charts for navigation.

NAVIGATION

The marked channel which flanks the western shore of Key Biscayne is an important passage for reaching Hawk Channel in the Atlantic, the main ocean route for traveling to the Keys. The channel follows the shoreline closely with noticeable shoals found to the southwest. There are also shoals off the tip of Cape Florida near the lighthouse. No Name Harbor is just off this channel and

ASHORE

The park lighthouse is open for tours and the adjoining beach is outstanding for sunbathing and swimming. Throughout the park you will find biking, hiking and skating paths along with attractive nature trails where native plant life has been restored. Fishing is a pastime of choice for anglers trying their luck from the seawalls along the Biscayne Bay side of the park. A concessionaire offers rentals of bicycles, kayaks, beach chairs and umbrellas.

Boaters making use of the harbor can visit the Boater's Grill in a two-story building with accompanying dockage for dinghies, however, do not expect much in the way of supplies for provisioning. Another open air restaurant, the Lighthouse Cafe, is found near the beach.

A northern anchorage off the Ragged Keys
of Biscayne Bay. The Boca Chita Key
lighthouse on Biscayne Bay (right).

ELLIOT KEY

In the southern waters of Biscayne Bay lies one of the largest keys in the park system that encompasses this large and vastly popular bay for boating. Elliott Key and surrounding islands, including Boca Chita Key, Soldier Key, the Ragged Keys and Old Rhodes Key are all part of the Biscayne National Park which is managed by the National Park Service.

Just a short day sail from Miami marinas, or a quick powerboat ride away, the waters of these keys are usually crowded with weekend boaters. During the week you will likely have your pick of secluded anchorages or slips in the two park marinas located on the keys. There are numerous outstanding anchorages throughout the park and they are excellent spots for overnighting while en route to southern destinations.

NAVIGATION

The waters within this park have numerous banks and shoals, so deeper draft craft do need to exercise some caution. The Featherbed Bank is a large area of shoaling that runs east and west across a good portion of this area. Marked channels lead boaters through both East and West Featherbed Banks. Consult your charts for details and for water depths at planned anchorages. It is worthy to note that the western shores of these islands are exposed and anchorages can become uncomfortable during any heavy weather.

ASHORE

The park service operates marinas on Boca Chita Key (see aerial photo on Page 7) and Elliott Key where you can overnight for modest fees that are paid to ATM-like machines. You will have to do without water or electric hookups, although at Elliott Key there are showers and drinking water is available. The marina here is limited to boats with drafts of three feet or less and larger vessels must anchor offshore and dinghy into the harbor.

Elliott Key has been maintained largely in a natural state, while other islands to the north were once privately owned. Boca Chita has a distinctive lighthouse structure at the entrance to the harbor. Besides picnicking, swimming off the beach, and snorkeling, visitors can also camp on these islands in designated areas. Fish life abounds in the cuts separating the islands and there are excellent fishing spots.

Sparkling clear waters, beaches and palm trees are all hallmarks of a Florida Keys vacation.

THE UPPER KEYS

The Card Sound Bridge leads from the
Florida mainland to North Key Largo.

BLACKWATER SOUND

Traveling along the ICW through Blackwater Sound and into Dusenbury and Grouper Creeks is always a special experience if you are departing from points north. You know at this junction that you have really arrived in the Keys. The waters are usually sparkling clear in the creeks and nearly always you'll find fishermen aboard small boats anchored along the shoreline hoping for snapper or even a grouper. As the route winds through these mangrove shores, it's almost impossible to believe the highway is just a stone's throw away with its traffic, stoplights, strip malls, tourist shops and fast food restaurants. Instead you can picture that this is the way you would like to see the Keys remain, and then realize it is wishful thinking.

NAVIGATION

There are no special challenges to navigating this area of the Intracoastal other than spotting markers and staying within the channel. If you have a draft in the five-foot range, you are likely to have some tense moments, but even boats drawing this much water should have little trouble. Keep a chart handy for reference and don't drift outside the channel. Slow down in the creeks and savor the moment, likewise, idle back for the many fishermen that you're bound to pass in these waters.

Anchoring possibilities abound throughout this area and it is possible to find secluded anchorages away from the hustle and bustle of nearby U.S. 1. Consult your charts and guides for suggestions.

ASHORE

While Blackwater Sound, Tarpon Basin, Buttonwood Sound and this area's backcountry offer outstanding anchorages, there is an acute lack of marinas that cater to the cruising boat traffic. Most marinas found along the northern stretches of Key Largo's bayside are small and the emphasis is on serving the owners of trailerable boats. This contrasts with the Atlantic side of Key Largo where there are several marinas off Hawk Channel that welcome the larger transient boats.

If you are planning on an extended stay in this section of the Keys, it is possible to find an anchorage where you can dinghy in for provisions and also to sample the many fine restaurants that are found here.

KEY LARGO

Key Largo, known as the diving capital of the world, is also home to the John Pennekamp Coral Reef State Park. This is the country's only underwater park and it has attracted millions of visitors since it was established in the 1960's. On first impression, the park grounds themselves appear quite small, but it is the real estate below the surface that encompasses more than 50,000 acres that is the park's real attraction and treasure. Divers and snorkelers will discover several hundred different species of fish and more than fifty types of coral making up the ecosystem of the park's coral reef. There are additionally a number of wrecks in the Key Largo area that are another attraction to divers.

KEY LARGO & LARGO SOUND

LARGO SOUND

Moorings

John Pennekamp Coral Reef State Park Headquarters & Marina

South Sound Creek

El Radabob Key

Atlantic Ocean

Shoals

NOT TO BE USED FOR NAVIGATION
Use as a reference only. Consult recommended charts for navigation.

NAVIGATION

Exercise care when operating your boat over these offshore reefs since there are shallow areas where you can easily run aground. This may cause damage to your vessel, but it is also bound to damage this fragile reef. You are responsible and fines can be extremely stiff for any damage to the reef, however accidental. Largo Sound does not allow anchoring and visiting boaters must take mooring provided by the park service. The moorings are available at a nominal fee and Largo Sound is a delightful spot for overnighting. When entering the South Sound Creek, keep aware of other boat traffic in this narrow channel and especially the park's large sightseeing vessel.

ASHORE

Besides the moorings offered in Largo Sound, the park does have a limited number of slips located in the marina, where the headquarters are also found. Camping is another favorite pastime on the grounds and there is a relaxing beach for sunbathing or swimming. Dive and snorkel tours of the reef and glass bottom boats leave frequently throughout the day from the park marina.

For those desiring a wide selection in restaurants, more landside activities and nightlife, there are a few marinas located just off Hawk Channel between the park and Rodriguez Key. They include Key Largo Harbour with a repair facility, Marina del Mar Resort and Marina, Pilot House Marina and Mandalay Marina. Call ahead to make sure dockage is available.

TAVERNIER HARBOR

In the heart of Tavernier on Key Largo is a popular anchorage known as Community Harbor that is simply reached from the Intracoastal Waterway running through Florida Bay. This is a well-protected natural harbor that for the large part is surrounded by mangroves and a marina complex to the southeast. Mangrove Marina is one of the few facilities along this section of the ICW that is equipped to truly handle transient or cruising boats. Most marinas along this route tend to be operations on the small side and largely cater to smaller boats. Mangrove Marina has more than 100 slips, electric, water and cable TV, a travel lift for haulouts, a ship's store and on site repairs. While the atmosphere could not be termed resort-style, it's a clean and quiet facility where renovation is continuing, and it is close to shopping and restaurants in Tavernier.

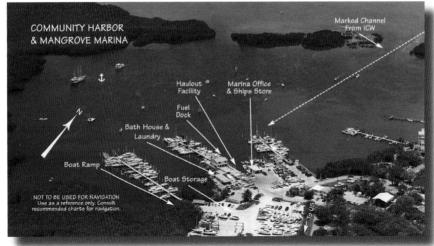

COMMUNITY HARBOR & MANGROVE MARINA

Marked Channel From ICW

Haulout Facility

Marina Office & Ships Store

Fuel Dock

Bath House & Laundry

Boat Ramp

Boat Storage

NOT TO BE USED FOR NAVIGATION
Use as a reference only. Consult recommended charts for navigation.

To US

NAVIGATION

If your boat draws over four feet, waters entering the Community Harbor may be a tight squeeze, especially at low tide. The entrance to this harbor is marked and is found a short distance on a southerly course from Marker 64. The entrance is narrow and shoals with a new growth of mangroves that flank the channel. Pay close attention to the markers and stay mid channel to enter the harbor. Once inside, you'll have the option of anchoring, or heading into the marina. As mentioned, the depths in this anchorage are on the shallow side, however, if you are able to navigate the ICW without problems, you should not have trouble here.

ASHORE

Tavernier is an interesting, small community with a hardware store, shops, small restaurants and restored homes and buildings, such as the Tavernier Hotel pictured below.

A short walk from the marina is a major shopping center with a supermarket, banking, fast food outlets, a cinema, video rentals, Dillon's Pub & Grill, a liquor store and post office. One of the Keys major hospitals, Mariners, is adjacent to the shopping center.

The backcountry waters of this area are also worthy of exploration as there are many interesting small islands and numerous anchoring possibilities for those wishing to be on the hook.

TAVERNIER CREEK

Tavernier Creek is a much used cut between Key Largo and Plantation Key connecting Florida Bay with the Atlantic. The western shore of this channel is heavily populated and packed with homes, while the opposite side remains largely mangroves. The creek is of no use to sailboats, or larger craft because of the fixed bridge spanning the channel. Regardless, traffic is usually heavy with small boats plying the channel on weekends.

Fishing and diving is excellent offshore along the reef here, and there are numerous dive shops and motels catering to the underwater fraternity. Molasses Reef, Conch and Little Conch, Hen and Chickens, Crocker Reef and Davis Reef are just offshore along Hawk Channel and are all popular for fishing, diving and snorkeling.

NAVIGATION

Reaching Tavernier Creek from Hawk Channel is simply accomplished and is straightforward. The channel is well-marked into the creek, but as can be seen from the photo, you must stay within the channel because of the shoaling. The fixed U.S. 1 bridge has a vertical clearance of only 15 feet and the current can be swift through the creek. On the opposite side, the channel winds through housing developments and mangroves until it eventually exits and intersects with the ICW. The markers at this intersection can be somewhat confusing, so utilize caution and study your charts if unfamiliar with the waters.

ASHORE

Partly because of the fixed bridge and additionally because there is not any transient dockage available along Tavernier Creek, this area holds little interest to cruising boaters traveling the Keys. However, it remains a hub of boating activity for smaller craft. The huge buildings of Tavernier Creek Marina house many boats in dry storage and on weekends and holidays it can be extremely busy here. Tavernier Creek Marina features a ship's store and gift shop, gas and diesel, the Las Brisas restaurant on the docks and Cuda's Bait & Tackle. Conch Republic Divers offer diving and snorkeling trips to the reef.

PLANTATION

Plantation Yacht Harbor has a lengthy history and this marina was once a favored destination for boaters cruising south to the Keys for a weekend or vacations. Major fishing tournaments were once staged from this facility. A few years ago it was purchased by the Village of Islamorada and the marina has been incorporated into the Islamorada Founders Park complex. This is a far cry from being the pineapple plantation that it once was in bygone years. Naturally, this transition has resulted in many changes, many which longtime visitors lament. In fact, the once popular lounge and restaurant is now Village Town Hall.

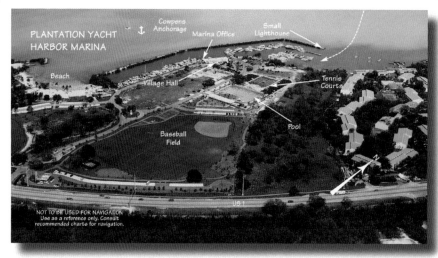

NAVIGATION

Conveniently located less than a mile from the ICW, Plantation Yacht Harbor has a landmark red and white lighthouse on the breakwater at the entrance to the marina. This breakwater provides for exceptional protection of the entire marina. Inside the harbor are about 80 slips, nearly all being permanent residents with only a handful of transient slips available. A good reason for reservations if you plan to visit here. Cowpens Anchor-age provides an alternative if you wish to drop the hook, however, this should only be considered only in fair weather as it is fairly exposed.

ASHORE

As mentioned, there is no longer a restaurant or lounge on the grounds. Other than the slips, the marina complex consists only of a dockmaster's office. You will be in need of transportation should you wish to reprovision or dine at any of the area restaurants.

Everything aside, this is an ideal destination for a cruise with the family, especially teenagers. The Founders Park is an impressive complex that provides a great deal of recreational pursuits. There is an olympic size, heated swimming pool, a baseball field, tennis and basketball courts and even a skateboard park.

Additionally the grounds feature an especially attractive beach with a swimming area. Here you can rent kayaks, sailboats or paddle boats. There is a playground, picnic areas and even a small dog park where you can unleash Fido for a run.

SNAKE CREEK

Snake Creek is an appropriate name for this winding channel that separates Windley Key and Plantation Key. There are several restaurants, bars and marinas along the channel's shores, but its real importance is that it is the first pass since the northern reaches of Key Largo where cruising vessels can pass from Florida Bay to the Atlantic without concern for clearance through low fixed bridges. It is an important passage for sailboats, large cruisers and sportfishing boats with towers.

NAVIGATION

Snake Creek is well-marked as you enter the channel from Hawk Channel on the oceanside. The channel does twist and turn as it leads towards the creek proper and shoals extend well out into the Atlantic. Depths are good throughout the channel and if you follow your markers accurately, you will have little problem navigating this passage.

The bascule bridge at U.S. 1 has 27 feet of vertical clearance, but opens on demand. Use care when approaching the bridge as you are likely to encounter strong currents during tidal changes.

On the opposite side of the bridge the channel forks and the marked route leads to the starboard with the intersection of the ICW just a short distance from the creek's mouth. Once in the bay you may wish to anchor with a number of possibilities available such as Cowpens Anchorage or at Cotton Key Basin.

ASHORE

Even though there are a number of marinas on Snake Creek, you are likely to find transient slips in short supply. Your best bet may be to try the Smuggler's Cove Marina immediately on the north side of the bridge. This is a small marina and resort with most of the slips taken up by permanent residents, which is mostly the case on this channel. The marina provides both gasoline and diesel, bait and tackle and limited supplies in a ship's store. Accommodations are available and there is a Tiki bar.

Another possibility is Cobra Marine across the channel and near the U.S. Coast Guard station. This marina has a limited number of transient slips and a ship's store.

There are a few dining options adjacent to the creek and one includes the Hog Heaven Bar and Restaurant. Hog Heaven, as the name implies attracts a good number of bikers.

WHALE HARBOR

Separating Windley Key and Upper Matecumbe Key, Whale Harbor Channel is a well traveled passage, especially on weekends. There are numerous backcountry and offshore fishing boats based at local marinas, as well as head boats that fish the Atlantic reefs. The well-known "Sandbar" that flanks the channel on both sides is a widely used party spot for boaters that can beach their craft on the sandy beaches for swimming, sunbathing and revelry.

The Holiday Isle Resort and Marina is the only facility in Whale Harbor that is transient friendly. The marina welcomes visiting boats, but again, reservations are strongly suggested at this popular destination. Across the channel, Whale Harbor Inn and Marina is largely occupied permanently by charter boats.

WHALE HARBOR CHANNEL

UPPER MATECUMBE KEY

Chesapeake Resort

Whale Harbor

Fixed Bridge Vert Cl 12 Ft
Hwy. US 1

Holiday Isle Dive Shop
Bimini Row Shops
Tiki Bar
Kokomo
Floater's Pool Bar
Cantina
RumRunners Beach

Mickey Rat's Bilge Bar
Ollie's Restaurant

Theater of
The Sea

RumRunners   Abel's

Pelican Cove

WINDLEY KEY

NOT TO BE USED FOR NAVIGATION
Use as a reference only. Consult
recommended charts for navigation.

NAVIGATION

From the ocean, navigation of the channel is straightforward through a well marked passage with adequate depths for most vessels. The Holiday Isle complex and its marina is entered from a channel to starboard just before the fixed bridge. Since this bridge only has a 12-foot clearance, any cruising boats must reach this port of call from the Atlantic. The northern side of the channel beyond the bridge is only suited for the flats fishing guides and center console boats. Alligator Reef Light, just offshore, is worthy of note since it is an outstanding snorkeling and diving site.

ASHORE

The Holiday Isle Resort is one of the Keys most popular stopovers for fun and relaxation. It is virtually an adult playground with several bars, regular live entertainment, beaches and swimming pools, watersports rentals and a number of restaurants that provide everything from hot dogs to steaks. The Tiki Bar and its Rum Runners are famous among Keys vacationers. The resort also provides accommodations for overnight stays and shoppers will find Bimini Row interesting. The Holiday Isle dive shop offers reef trips for snorkelers and divers, and anglers have a wide range of fishing options.

Across the bridge spanning the channel is the Whale Harbor Inn and Restaurant, which specializes in seafood and waterfront dining. Here you will find another landmark, the Chesapeake Resort featuring oceanfront accommodations and beaches.

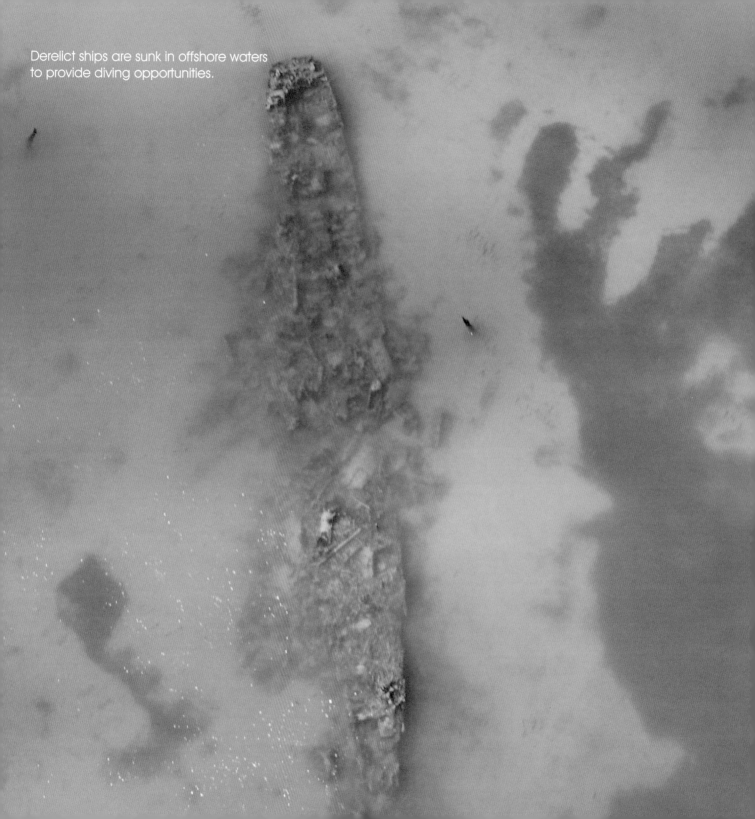

Derelict ships are sunk in offshore waters to provide diving opportunities.

THE MIDDLE KEYS

Whale Harbor

LITTLE BASIN, ISLAMORADA

Little Basin on Upper Matecumbe Key is a popular anchorage among cruising boaters since it is well protected, easily reached from the ICW and is close to a wide range of restaurants, shops and galleries, attractions and grocery stores. As part of the Village of Islamorada, which takes in several keys and towns, Upper Matecumbe also features a number of marina facilities that cater to transient boaters. Islamorada, which translates into the purple isles in Spanish, bills itself as the fishing capital of the world. Throughout the waters surrounding this sprawling community you will always find fishermen on the flats, or aboard boats headed towards offshore fishing grounds. Additionally, here you will find several of the Keys most famous resorts, such Cheeca Lodge and The Islander.

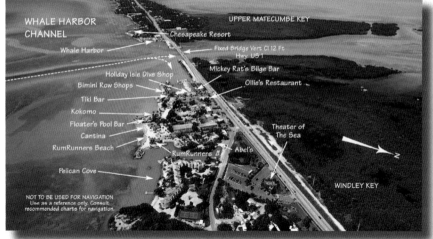

WHALE HARBOR CHANNEL
Whale Harbor
Holiday Isle Dive Shop
Bimini Row Shops
Tiki Bar
Kokomo
Floater's Pool Bar
Cantina
RumRunners Beach
Pelican Cove
NOT TO BE USED FOR NAVIGATION.
Use as a reference only. Consult recommended charts for navigation.
UPPER MATECUMBE KEY
Chesapeake Resort
Fixed Bridge Vert Cl 12 Ft Hwy. US 1
Mickey Rat's Bilge Bar
Ollie's Restaurant
Theater of The Sea
RumRunners
Abel's
WINDLEY KEY

NAVIGATION

The entrance to Little Basin and its waters are on the shallow side. World Wide Sportsman Marina personnel recommend taking up a course of 163 degrees at Marker 84 on the ICW. At the entrance you will find Markers 1 and 2 leading into Little Basin. Inside depths range from three and a half to five feet at low tide and there is about a foot and a half tidal difference. This is a popular spot for anchoring for shallower draft boat owners. If you don't wish to dinghy ashore, head into the docks at World Wide Sportsman's Bayside Marina.

ASHORE

The World Wide Sportsman two-story complex is virtually a Disney World for the angler and boater. Here you will find aisles and display cases featuring the finest in sportfishing rods and reels, lures, books, clothing and sporting art. The centerpiece of the main floor is occupied by the sister ship to the famed Ernest Hemingway's sportfishing vessel the *Pilar*. It has been beautifully restored and you can step aboard and visualize how sportfishing has changed in recent years.

Next door is the Islamorada Fish Company which offers inside or marina front dining. Along U.S. 1 are numerous excellent restaurants including Sid & Roxie's famed Green Turtle Inn and Chep Lupe's Lazy Days. Other dining spots serve dishes ranging from sushi to Spanish or Italian cuisine. The nearby Lorelei Restaurant and Cabana Bar is a favorite gathering place for watching sunsets and for backcountry captains and anglers.

UPPER MATECUMBE KEY

Bud N' Mary's Marina is one of the most famous destinations when it comes to sportfishing. The marina has been well-known for years as one of the best spots to charter a boat for offshore fishing in search of sailfish, dolphin, kingfish and reef fish. It is home to a sizeable charterboat fleet operated by some of the Key's most capable and productive captains. Waters offshore of Upper Matecumbe are noted for their outstanding angling prospects. Likewise, the backcountry is equally favorable for bonefish, tarpon, snook, redfish and other gamefish species. This marina also has numerous flats fishing guides available for this style of fishing. There is also no shortage of offshore charterboats based along these middle Keys if you are in search of sailfish, dolphin, or other pelagic species.

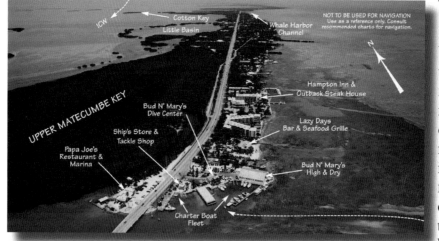

NAVIGATION

Again, another fixed bridge here with only 10 feet of vertical clearance limits passage from the bayside to skiffs. Access to this marina must be made from the ocean into a marked channel leading into the two separate harbor areas. Indian Key Channel with a high bridge is located nearby to the west for boats traveling from Florida Bay.

There are anchoring or mooring possibilities at Indian Key, Lignumvitae Key and Shell Key. All three islands are part of the state parks system.

ASHORE

Although almost with certainty all the emphasis here is on fishing, there are a number of restaurants of interest. The best known is another Keys landmark, Papa Joe's across the street from Bud N' Mary's. Diners have been frequenting this establishment for many years and it is one of the few old time Keys-style restaurants remaining. Hundreds of fishing pictures decorate the walls of the dining room and lounge adding to the nostalgic atmosphere. Papa Joe's has a small marina, an upper deck lounge and boat rentals. Two other restaurants within walking distance are the Outback Steak House in the Hampton Inn and Lazy Day Bar and Seafood Grille. Besides accommodations at Bud N' Mary's, the Hampton Inn provides rooms and there are several other oceanfront resorts.

The Bud N' Mary's complex has an on site dive center offering reef diving and snorkeling trips, boat rentals and a fine bait and tackle shop also carrying ship's supplies.

INDIAN KEY CHANNEL

O
f all the islands in the Keys, Indian Key has among the most historic, bloody and truly fascinating pasts. It has been home to native American Indians, a thriving community was once built here largely based on the wrecking trade, it was once designated as the Dade County seat of government, it was the site of a massacre, once a home to a famed botanist and ultimately it has become part of Florida's state park system. Its history is so colorful that it could be scripted as a movie.

More can be learned about the island's past by taking a tour, and while there is not a great deal to see, learning more about Indian Key is worthwhile. Stop by Robbie's Marina at the tip of Lower Matecumbe Key for tour information to both Indian Key and Lignumvitae Key, another interesting state park island.

NAVIGATION

Indian Key Channel is well-marked as it snakes through shoals and banks on both sides of the bridge. If you pay attention to the channel aids and utilize your eyesight for navigating, it poses no problems as a passage. A fixed bridge at 27 feet unfortunately limits use of the channel.

Anchorages and moorings are found at both Lignumvitae and Indian Keys. Visitors to either island can also use guest dockage that is largely dependent upon your draft. Lignumvitae Channel to the west is only suited for smaller boats since it has a fixed bridge with only 10 feet of clearance.

ASHORE

A visit to Robbie's Marina on Lignumvitae Channel is entertaining just to take in the spectacle of huge tarpon, numbering in the hundreds, virtually being hand fed. Over the years the tarpon have been attracted to the docks by this handout and their aggressive feeding is a sight to see. For a small fee you can buy a bucket of bait and take part.

Robbie's is a small marina and takes transient boats, but slips are usually limited. Make reservations ahead of time if you hope to visit with your own boat. This marina is popular among boat trailering fishermen and there are accommodations nearby. Kayaks and other boats can be rented and there is a restaurant appropriately named the Hungry Tarpon that serves three meals a day adjacent to the marina.

LOWER MATECUMBE KEY

There are few marinas in the Keys that offer the immediate access to the ocean that is found at Caloosa Cove Marina, and it's one of the reasons it is popular among charterboat captains and small craft fishermen. The building for dry storage at this marina is painted with an interesting mural featuring a scene depicting life among the Indians who once populated these islands. The painting is extremely well done and must have presented a sizeable challenge for the artist. It overlooks the small harbor which is home to several charter vessels.

NAVIGATION

The channel leading into the marina is well-marked, deep, and navigation is straight forward from Hawk Channel. Unfortunately a fixed bridge at Channel Two limits passage to Florida Bay to only back-country boats. However, just a short distance to the west is Channel Five, which represents one of the most important passages in the Lower Keys for transiting back and forth between the ocean and Florida Bay waters. Channel Five is an easily navigated passage with deep water and a bridge with a vertical clearance of 65 feet. This channel is adjacent to Long Key Bight on the ocean, which offers

LOWER MATECUMBE KEY — Channel Five — Channel Two — True Value Hardware — Caloosa Cove Marina — Bait & Tackle Shop — Convenience Store — Captain's Table Restaurant — Safari Lounge — Beach — Caloosa Cove Oceanfront Resort — U.S. 1 — NOT TO BE USED FOR NAVIGATION Use as a reference only. Consult recommended charts for navigation. — N

possibilities for anchoring. Fiesta Key is nearby, and although this is an RV park, there is also a marina that accepts transient boats. Another anchorage can be found in Matecumbe harbor in Florida Bay.

ASHORE

If you have a desire to stay ashore for a night, Caloosa Cove Resort adjoining the marina offers luxury oceanfront accommodations in 30 condominiums, complete with a large pool, a small beach and tennis courts. The Safari Lounge overlooks the ocean with grand views from its patio and features a unique decor with many mounted trophies and photographs that were taken during African safaris. The lounge offers package goods. For breakfast, lunch and dinner visit the Captain's Table on the marina grounds.

As a part of this complex there is additionally a well-stocked bait and tackle shop, a convenience store and a TrueValue Hardware shop that has many marine supplies. Boats can be rented from the marina.

Across U.S. 1 is the Florida National High Adventure Sea Base connected with the Boy Scouts.

DUCK KEY

Duck Key is home to one of the Keys most well known vacation facilities, Hawk's Cay Resort and Marina, a huge complex that offers visitors a luxurious life-style that rivals any on the mainland. With its close proximity to the ocean waters for sportfishing and diving or snorkeling, the 85-slip Hawk's Cay Marina has long been a choice port of call for boaters traveling to the Keys. Much of this small island is occupied by high end homes and it lacks the commercialism that is so evident throughout much of the Keys. The grounds of the island are meticulously kept and the atmosphere is more akin to what you might find in Palm Beach rather than the laid-back Keys. There is a wealth of watersports programs available including Colgate's Offshore Sailing School, offshore and backcountry fishing charters, boat and watercraft rentals, daily cruises, parasailing and snorkeling and diving instruction or excursions from Tilden's Scuba Center. Combine this with several restaurants, a number of lounges and top shelf accommodations, and you will find visitors are likely to discover they have little desire to leave the island while vacationing.

DUCK KEY & HAWK'S CAY RESORT & MARINA
Toms Harbor Keys
Duck Key Marina
Hawk's Cay Main Marina
NOT TO BE USED FOR NAVIGATION
Use as a reference only. Consult recommended charts for navigation.
WatersEdge Restaurant
U.S. 1
Dolphin Connection At Hawk's Cay
Small Boat Basin
The Inn At Hawk's Cay
Enter Channel From Ocean
N

NAVIGATION

For most boaters, the only route to approach the marina is from Hawks Channel since bridges from Florida Bay are very limited in vertical clearance, the exception being the bridge at Channel Five at the north end of Long Key. From the ocean a privately marked channel leads into the marina traveling between a breakwater to the starboard and homes to the port. The current can be swift in the channel. Hail the marina on VHF 16 should you have questions. Reservations are also advised at this popular port of call.

ASHORE

The marina features an outstanding ship's store and most of the resort's watersports concessions are located along the docks. The Waters Edge restaurant and lounge overlooks the marina. Nearby is the Duck Key Plaza which has a bank, a realtor, the Duck Key Emporium deli and All That Glitters jewelry store. That's largely the extent of your shopping prospects on the island, other than resort shops.

Duck Key Marina is another boating facility on the island and it caters largely to smaller boats. It has a ship's store, service and parts department, a dry storage barn, fuel and offers boat rentals.

KEY COLONY

Coco Plum Beach and Key Colony Beach are heavily residential areas with a good number of motels and beachfront resorts scattered throughout the communities. There is little opportunity for anchoring in this section of the Keys and slips for transient cruising boats are likely to be in short supply.

Nonetheless, should you be able to find dockage, this is a pleasant stopover on a Keys cruise. It is a quiet community with a few restaurants and shops, and it is close to Marathon for airport transportation, grocery stores, provisioning and marine supply stores.

NAVIGATION

Accessed from Hawk Channel on the Atlantic, an easily spotted landmark for the cut entrance is the high-rise Bonefish Towers condominium building. This building can be spotted from a good distance away and is located on the eastern shore of the channel leading into Key Colony Beach. Another channel that is widely utilized for crossing from the ocean to the bayside waters is Vaca Cut, however, a fixed bridge limits the size of a vessel making the passage. Waters within the harbor are shallow and not suited to anchoring by deeper draft vessels.

ASHORE

The first possibility for dockage when entering the channel is at the Bonefish Marina, and while these slips are privately owned, sometimes space is available with prior arrangements. Farther into the harbor you will find the Key Colony Beach Marina. The marina offers transient slips and features a tackle shop boat rentals and fuel. A Deep Blue Dive Center is located on the premises and the Quarterdeck Restaurant serves lunch and dinner. Adjacent to the marina is a strip mall with limited groceries available and a deli. Small boat dockage can be found at the Holiday Inn Marina if you are a hotel guest, and adjoining the facility is the Abyss Dive Center.

Just to the west before reaching Marathon is Vaca Cut pictured below. The current is usually swift through this channel, so be prepared. The Boat House Marina to starboard caters mostly to smaller boats with a large high and dry facility. Just before the bridge to the port is Captain Hook's Marina (both shown below), however, there are no transient slips available. This is a dive operation and fishing center for charter and party boats.

VACA KEY — Vaca Cut — Boat House Marina — Island Tiki Bar & Restaurant — Captain Hook's Marina & Dive Center — Key Colony Beach Marina & Charter Fleet — KEY COLONY — Quarterdeck Restaurant — Bonefish Marina — Bonefish Towers — Coco Plum Beach — COCO PLUM BEACH & KEY COLONY BEACH — NOT TO BE USED FOR NAVIGATION Use as a reference only. Consult recommended charts for navigation.

MARATHON

Boot Key Harbor in the heart of Marathon has long been one of the most heavily populated harbors in the Florida Keys. It is well protected and does accommodate a great number of cruising and liveaboard boats, especially during the winter months. However, along with the harbor's popularity has arisen some controversy. There are efforts being made to "clean up" the atmosphere and crack down on those who violate overboard waste laws. Anchoring may one day become a life-style of the past in the harbor with increasing emphasis being placed on paid moorings. There is never likely to be a happy or equitable solution, but meanwhile life goes on in this colorful community of cruisers.

room and make sure your anchor is firmly planted in case of a blow. You are certain to have a great deal of company.

ASHORE

Boot Key Harbor features several excellent marinas with a wide variety of amenities and several are mentioned accompanying the smaller photo below. Farther into the harbor you will find the Boot Key Harbor City Marina, which also offers pumpouts and dinghy dockage, the Sombrero Marina and Dockside Lounge, and the Sombrero Resort and Lighthouse Marina. The Dockside Lounge provides excellent food, live entertainment every

evening of the week, and is the favorite gathering spot for cruisers and liveaboards. You'll find a resort atmosphere with a pool, tennis courts, accommodations, a tiki bar, restaurant and gift shop at the Sombrero Resort and Lighthouse Marina. Sombrero Reef Explorers is the on site dive shop offering private snorkeling trips as well as sunset cruises.

Throughout Marathon are a wide spectrum of restaurants, enough to satisfy any dining desires. Marine supplies and repair services are readily available.

NAVIGATION

The harbor can be entered through two channels, one at Sister Creek on the oceanside and the other to the west at the beginning of the Seven Mile Bridge. The channels are well-marked, but take some unexpected turns, and if you are visiting for the first time, consult your charts. Once inside the harbor, you will discover some shoal areas and efforts to rebuild seagrass beds. Should you plan on anchoring out, try to find a spot with adequate swing

Pigeon Key near Marathon.

THE LOWER KEYS

A catamaran sailboat sets out from Key West Harbor.

Secluded anchorages are one of the factors making the Florida Keys attractive for cruising. Channel Key is popular.

Fly fishing on the colorful flats.

BAHIA HONDA KEY

Bahia Honda Florida State Park is one of the finest facilities of its kind that you will find in the Keys, or for that matter the mainland. It occupies around 500 acres and was once part of Henry Flagler's East Coast Railway project that began in 1905. A new bridge now serves travelers on U.S. 1, but at the park a portion of the Old Bahia Honda Bridge has been preserved and offers visitors a dramatic viewing post overlooking the Atlantic Ocean and Florida Bay.

With miles of some of the best beaches found in the Keys, the park offers outstanding swimming, snorkeling and beachcombing. Additionally overnight lodging is available, camping, bicycling, fishing, picnicking, kayaking and there is a marina. It is a widely utilized park among visitors and residents of the Keys alike.

NAVIGATION

Bahia Honda Channel is one of the deepest natural passages in the Keys and it is a good choice for moving between the Atlantic waters and Florida Bay, unless you are a sailboat or other vessel that requires more than 20 feet of clearance. The newly constructed bridge is fixed at this vertical clearance, however, the good news is a portion of the old bridge has been cut away to allow boats into an anchorage between the spans with access to the park. This anchorage can be a bit rough in some weather conditions, and it is worth noting that the current can be extremely swift. As shown in the photo, another anchorage on the bayside may be more protected, depending upon wind direction and strength.

ASHORE

The park is ideally suited for just relaxing along the beach shores under the shade of a palm tree or sunbathing in the sand. Because of the shallow waters surrounding much of the park, it is perfect for snorkeling and swimming from the shore. The flats found along the shoreline are great for the wading fly fisherman.

The park marina does provide dockage for transient boats in a well-protected harbor with 30 amp electricity, waste pump out and water. A concession building is a short walk and here you will find bait and tackle, a limited supply of groceries, gifts, a snack bar and ice. A tour boat offers daily snorkeling trips to Looe Key reef.

Another marina accepting transients is Sunshine Key, immediately to the northeast.

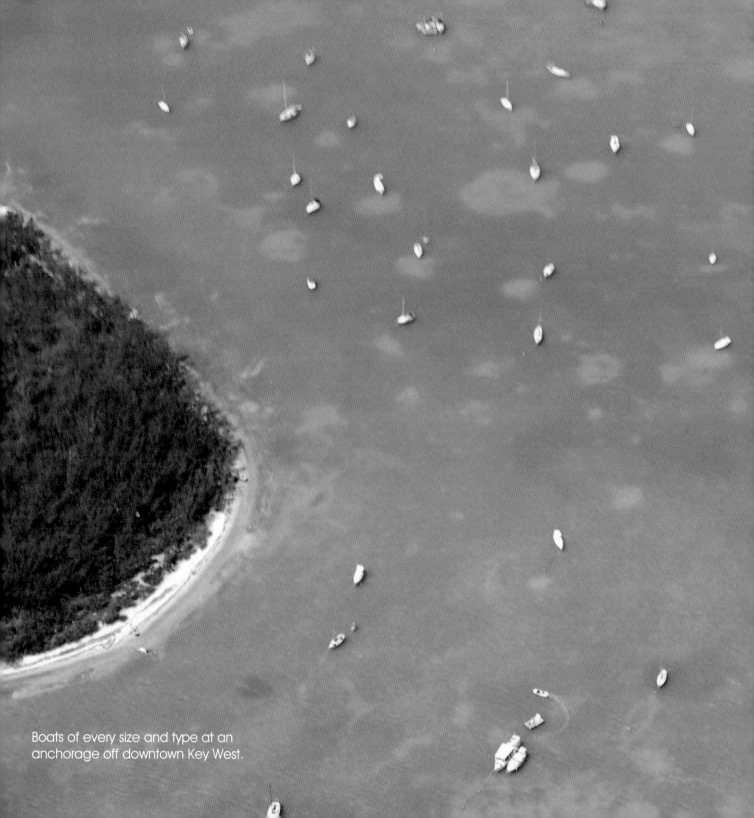

Boats of every size and type at an anchorage off downtown Key West.

A span of an old U.S. 1 bridge has been removed
for sailboat passages at Bahia Honda State Park.

NEWFOUND HARBOUR

The upper reaches of Newfound Harbor Channel offer several fine anchoring prospects for boats traveling on the Atlantic side along Hawk Channel, however dockage in this region is somewhat limited. This is especially true for deeper draft vessels.

There are attractions that make a visit to this area worthwhile, including the nearby the Looe Key National Marine Sanctuary which is regarded as one of the premier diving and snorkeling sites in the Keys. Named for the H.M.S. Looe, a British ship wrecked in the 1700's, it is known for incredible staghorn coral formations that are found nearly at the water's surface. Deeper canyons abound throughout the coral making this dive ideal for both beginners and advanced divers alike.

It will require auto transportation, but a visit to the Key Deer National Wildlife Refuge on Big Pine Key and No Name Key should be considered. Here you will discover the endangered Key deer that stand at only a couple of feet tall.

NAVIGATION

Newfound Harbor Channel is easily navigated and

NEWFOUND HARBOR CHANNEL & LITTLE PALM ISLAND

NOT TO BE USED FOR NAVIGATION
Use as a reference only. Consult recommended charts for navigation.

Newfound Harbor Keys

To Hawk Channel

Little Palm Island

Shoals

N

anchorages can be found in Newfound Harbor and along the shores of both Little Torch Key to the Port and Big Pine Key to starboard. The channel provides fair protection in most weather conditions.

ASHORE

Immediately upon entering the channel, Little Palm Island will be found to the starboard. This once was the site of a fishing camp that had hosted a number of U.S. presidents and other notables, as well as being used for the filming of the movie PT 109. It is now the exclusive Little Palm Island Resort & Spa and can only be reached by boat or seaplane. Accommodations are available in 28 thatched roof bungalows on the shores of the island, and the resort restaurant is known for its gourmet dining. Guests and visitors are ferried from a facility on Little Torch Key.

Cruising craft with a modest draft can be accommodated overnight at the Dolphin Resort and Marina on Little Torch Key just before the 15-foot fixed bridge for U.S. 1. The Keys Sea Center is another marina located across the channel on Big Pine Key, however, it caters to smaller boats and does not have slips for transients.

Colorful houseboats in Garrison Bight offer a unique style of living.

Key West's beaches draw
crowds every day of the week.

STOCK ISLAND

Stock Island lacks the glamor and glitz of its neighboring Key West and is more of a "working man's" island. On first impression this community is a hodgepodge of warehouses, trailer parks, commercial docks filled with lobster and stone crab boats, boat builders, convenience stores and other buildings. All of this contrasts sharply with the high dollar condominiums which border the ocean.

Stock Island has humble beginnings and history records the island was utilized as a stockyard of sorts for barnyard animals that were ultimately served up on menus in Key West. You can grow tired of seafood.

Appearances aside, Stock Island does feature one of the finest boating facilities in the Keys, Oceanside Marina, and an excellent boatyard, especially for do-it-yourselfers, Peninsular Marine Enterprises. Likewise, there are numerous other small shops scattered throughout the island which specialize in providing supplies and services for the boater.

ASHORE

Oceanside Marina caters to cruising boaters and the facility is second to none, however, sportfishing is likewise taken very seriously here. In fact, Oceanside is home to more world record gamefish catches than any marina in the country. It is also an important stepping off point for Cuba, Mexico or points south in the Caribbean. There is fuel on site, a ship's store with bait and tackle, huge dry storage barns, boat ramps and showers. Adjoining the Oceanside complex are boating related businesses and the Florida Keys Boat Center. The Peninsular boatyard is within walking distance and is a widely utilized yard among cruisers.

Two Stock Island restaurants that deserve note are the Rusty Anchor and Hickory House. The Rusty Anchor is part of a commercial seafood operation and you can depend on your seafood choices to be caught that day. The restaurant is a favorite among Key West locals. Hickory House is across the street from Oceanside Marina and features a Keys character served up with excellent food and a comfortable lounge.

Sunset Marina, not shown in these aerial photos, is a new marina located on the Gulf side of Stock Island. This marina provides transient and permanent dockage, a grocery store, fuel, a marine service shop and other amenities.

KEY WEST

Key West has a wide diversity of cultures, a rich and fascinating history, sparkling clear waters, beaches, wide choices in dining, exciting nightlife and many attractions that make this city one of the country's most popular vacation destinations. Key West is literally at the end of the road, being the southernmost city in the U.S., and it is closer in proximity to Havana than Miami.

Because of its colorful flavor and climate, Key West has attracted many literary and creative types in years past included famed writers Ernest Hemingway, Tennessee Williams and Robert Frost. Among other notable individuals, President Harry Truman vacationed in the "Little White House" located on Front Street. While popular among vacationers, Key West is an equally desirable destination for cruising boaters, sportfishermen and divers. Prior reservations for dockage at the local marinas are most often a must.

NAVIGATION
Key West Harbor is reached from the ocean by a well-marked, deep and wide Main Ship's Channel. This is negotiated by large cruise ships and poses little challenge after consulting your charts. For those traveling from Gulf of Mexico waters, Northwest Channel represents the favored passage.

ASHORE
Entire books have been published on visiting Key West, and the bars, restaurants, attractions, museums, and hotels are much too numerous to mention here. However, regardless of your interests, dining pleasures or plans for a night on the town, you can count on finding it in Key West. Visit the Chamber of Commerce for maps and other information. Don't miss the tradition of the sunset party at Mallory Square on the waterfront, and if you want to take in much of the city in a short time, board one of the many trolleys or Conch Trains that journey throughout the neighboring streets.

If you are not planning on anchoring out, or taking a city mooring, you have a choice of several marinas including the Conch Harbor Marina, the Galleon Marina, A & B Marina, Key West Bight Marina, and the Hilton Key West Resort and Marina, which are all located within walking distance of downtown. Other choices include marinas centered around the Garrison Bight area

KEY WEST BIGHT

Key West Bight was once the center of a thriving shrimp industry and much of the bight's dockage and waterfront was occupied by hundreds of shrimp boats that were berthed here.

The city bought much of the property in the Bight in the early 90's and it has since been transformed into an attraction in itself, Key West's Historic Seaport and Harborwalk. The shrimping fleet has since relocated to Safe Harbor on Stock Island. The maritime flavor surrounding the Bight has been preserved since it has become the home port for a number of classic vessels and tall ships, all of which provide visitors with a wide variety of cruises. The Seaport is the base for much of the city's fishing charter fleet, sailing, snorkeling and diving excursions and ferry boat services to the Dry Tortugas plus high-speed round-trip ferries between Fort Myers, Miami and Key West.

KEY WEST BIGHT & HISTORIC SEAPORT

Ferry Terminal

City Marina

NOT TO BE USED FOR NAVIGATION. Use as a reference only. Consult recommended charts for navigation.

Conch Harbor Marina

Schooner Wharf

Turtle Kraal

A&B Marina

Waterfront Market

The Galleon Marina

Conch Republic Seafood

The Galleon

NAVIGATION

The Key West Bight Channel is deep and wide and presents no navigational challenges, however, you can expect heavy traffic throughout the Bight on almost any day, and especially weekends. Besides the recreational vessels, there are the many tourism oriented craft and commercial boats that utilize the waters of the Bight at all times of the day.

ASHORE

The Seaport boasts several waterfront restaurants and bars including the Conch Republic Seafood Company, Half Shell Raw Bar, Turtle Kraals and Schooners Wharf Bar. Most provide live music and you can always count on lively crowds most afternoons and evenings.

Shoppers won't be disappointed since there are several interesting shops and galleries on the waterfront, and the Waterfront Market is well-known for its seafood, produce and deli. Numerous events, such as Key West Race Week and the Conch Republic Independence Celebration, are staged from this harbor.

Visiting boaters should always make reservations well in advance for berths as dockage is in high demand at the popular marinas which include the Galleon Marina, a resort-style complex, the A&B Marina, Conch Harbor Marina, and the City Marina at Key West Bight. The Seaport is the hub of a great deal of Key West's activities and these marinas put you in the heart of the action.

MARQUESAS KEYS

For cruisers with an adventurous streak and those who are seeking the solitude and beauty of almost untouched islands, a visit to the Boca Grande and Marquesas Keys is especially worthwhile. This group of keys are also a logical stopover for anyone cruising to the Dry Tortugas and Fort Jefferson since this destination is about 70 miles from Key West. But this is not all without sacrifice because you will be leaving the comfort of docks and electricity, grocery stores and restaurants, fuel and ice all behind in Key West. These keys are much like they would have been found hundreds of years ago and they are largely unspoiled.

A visit here requires a good deal of prior planning, and careful consideration as weather conditions must be heeded because there are few places safely providing shelter during frequent blows which sweep these islands.

Channel heading west along the chain of islands on the ocean side, or via the northern route along the Northwest Channel. Weather at the time will dictate which route is the best for your voyage. Detailed charts and the advice offered by other Keys guides are essential for navigating these waters. Good light is also helpful for spotting channel markers, heads and shoals.

The anchorage for Boca Grande Key is located in the channel at the northwestern reaches of the island. Mooney Harbor in the Marquesas Keys offers other anchoring options. Use a good deal of care when entering either of these anchorages by keeping a sharp lookout and studying charts. As mentioned, neither of these destinations are safely navigated or suitable for anchoring in any heavy weather or poor visibility.

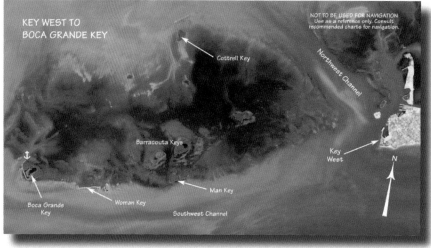

KEY WEST TO BOCA GRANDE KEY

NOT TO BE USED FOR NAVIGATION
Use as a reference only. Consult recommended charts for navigation.

Cottrell Key

Northwest Channel

Barracouta Keys

Key West

N

Man Key

Boca Grande Key

Woman Key

Southwest Channel

NAVIGATION

As is evident from the two accompanying satellite images, these keys are surrounded by shoals, reef formations, coral heads and meandering channels that often dead end. Anchorages at Boca Grande Key and the Marquesas Keys can either be reached from Hawk

ASHORE

This group of keys are noted for its excellent flats fishing including permit, bonefish and tarpon. There is also excellent snorkeling and exploration aboard your dinghy. The anchorages can also be "buggy", so be prepared.

A dramatic satellite view of an island in the Marquesas group.

The Marquesas group of islands between Key West and the Dry Tortugas are unspoiled and ideal for cruising.

FORT JEFFERSON

Steeped in a colorful history, a visit to Dry Tortugas and Fort Jefferson represents a fascinating step back into time. This group of islands, laying approximately 70 miles west of Key West was discovered by the Spanish explorer Ponce de Leon in 1513 and were named "Las Tortugas" (the turtles) because of their population of sea turtles. "Dry" was later added to their name warning sailors of a lack of water.

In 1825 a lighthouse was first built on Garden Key and construction of Fort Jefferson began in 1846 and continued for 30 years. The fort was never completely finished, however, it is remarkably well preserved and has been declared a national monument.

GARDEN KEY & FORT JEFFERSON

FORT JEFFERSON

Park & Ferry Docks

NOT TO BE USED FOR NAVIGATION
Use as a reference only. Consult recommended charts for navigation.

The Dry Tortugas were designated as a national park more than a decade ago.

The only means of reaching this park is either aboard your own boat, high speed ferries, or seaplanes departing on a regular basis from the Key West.

NAVIGATION

Cruisers setting out for the popular anchorage at Garden Key have a choice of a northerly route along Northwest Channel or the southerly Atlantic passage from Southwest Channel. Weather will often be the deciding factor for which route will be the most comfortable or fastest. Consult your guides and charts, but be sure to leave yourself enough time to reach the Dry Tortugas in daylight hours before anchoring up for the night. Channels leading into the Garden Key anchorage are well marked.

A self-guided tour of Fort Jefferson is a must for any visitor and park personnel are especially helpful. After taking in the fort, you have your choice of sunbathing on the spectacular beaches, or diving into the crystal clear waters and enjoying some of the finest snorkeling that can be found anywhere. Birdwatching is another favorite pastime as up to 200 different varieties can be spotted on the islands during various times of the year. As you would expect for a more remote area, the fishing is outstanding.

If you are cruising to these landmark and unique keys, once you have arrived, it is recommended to check in with a park ranger and inquire about restrictions regarding anchoring, fishing, diving and spearfishing. Certain activities are highly regulated in these environmentally sensitive islands.

Fort Jefferson and its anchorage in the Dry Tortugas.
Photo Seaplanes of Key West

Fort Jefferson is open to visitors by boat or seaplane and has a colorful history.

Tarpon, or the silver king, are one of the most highly regarded gamefish found in the Florida Keys.

Made in the USA
Lexington, KY
11 January 2014